Art For The Heart

Art therapy coloring book For Adults

Dedicated to my love, Serean

By Denise Trifonoff

© 2018 Denise Trifonoff

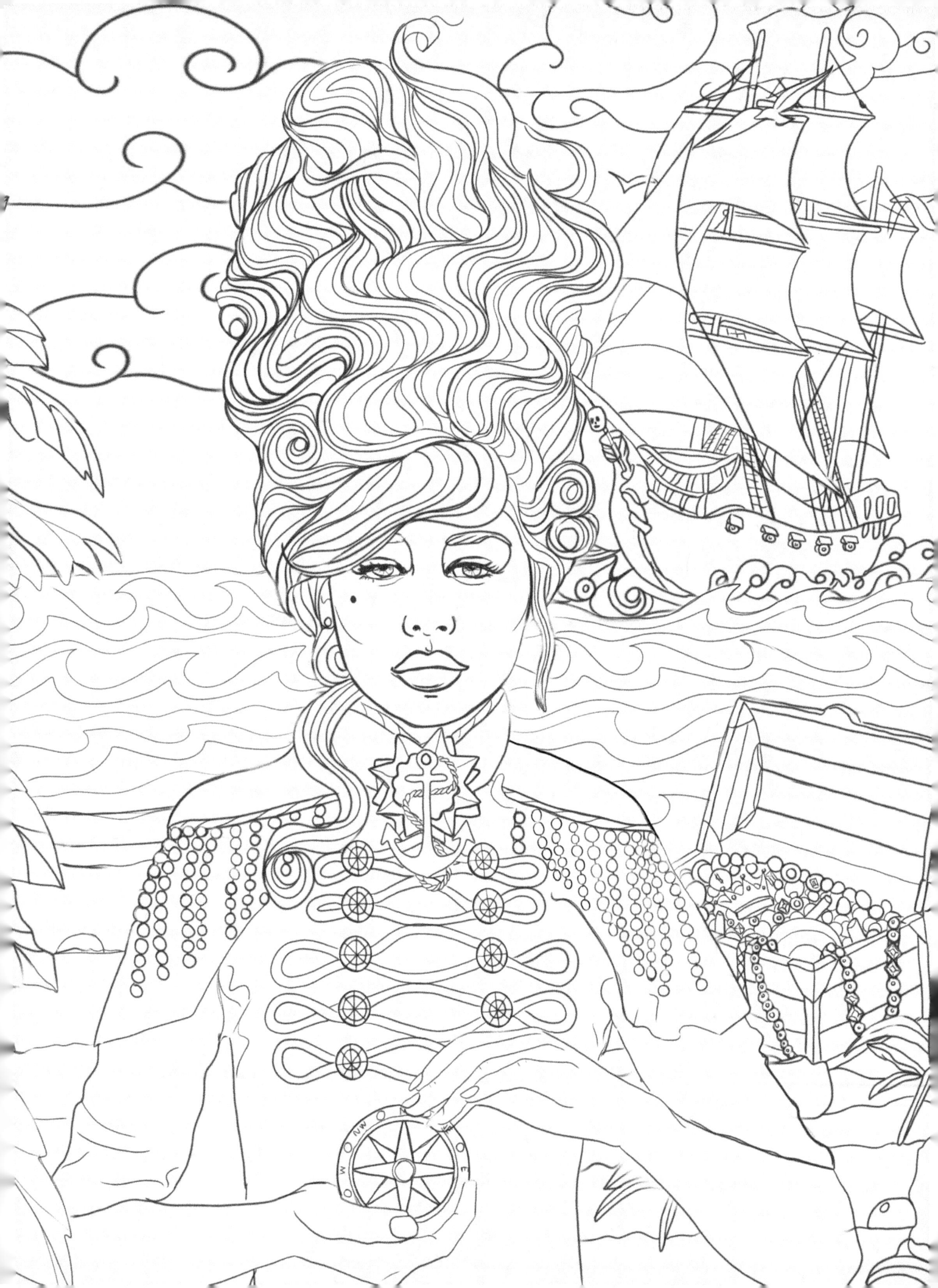

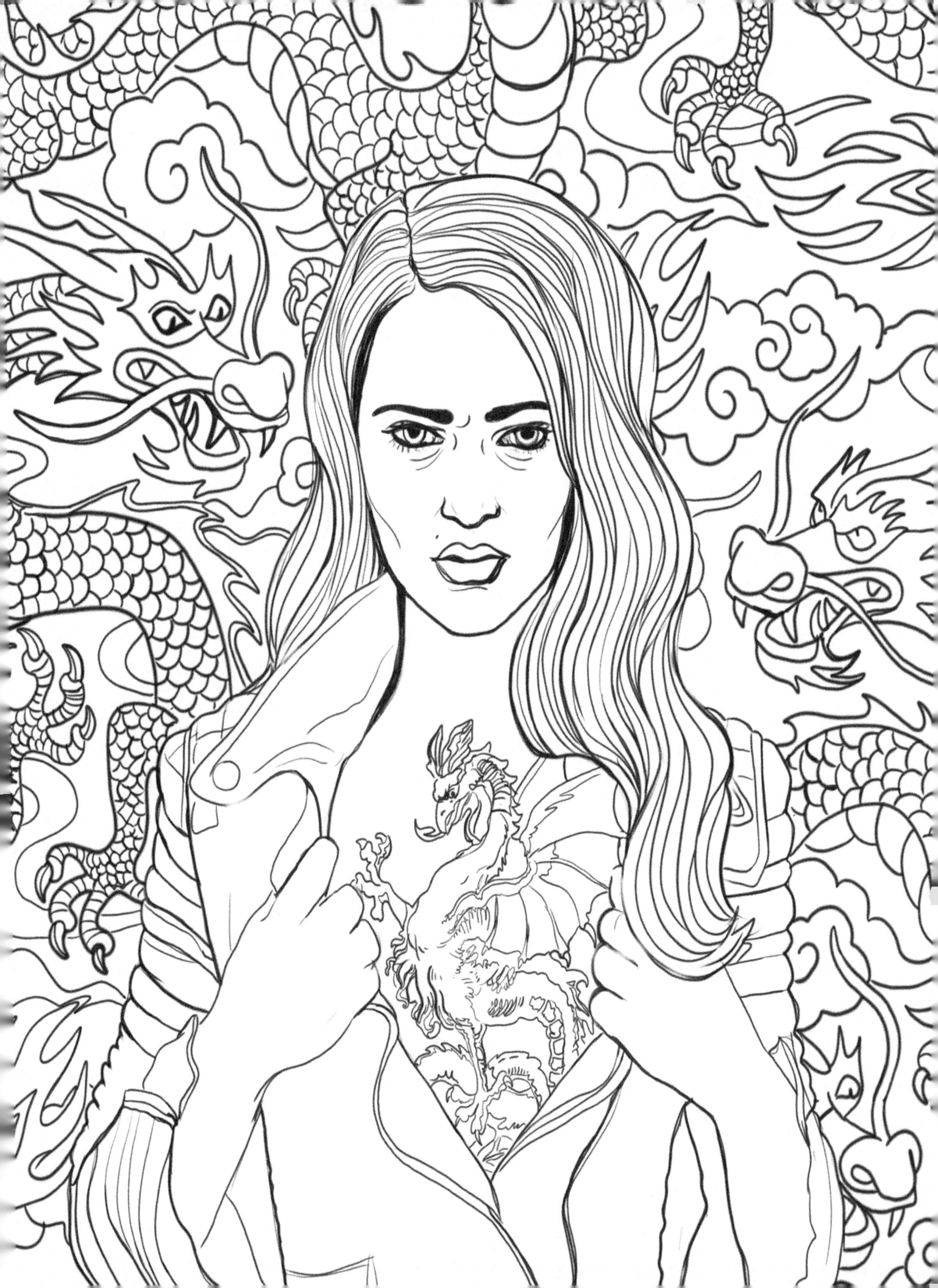

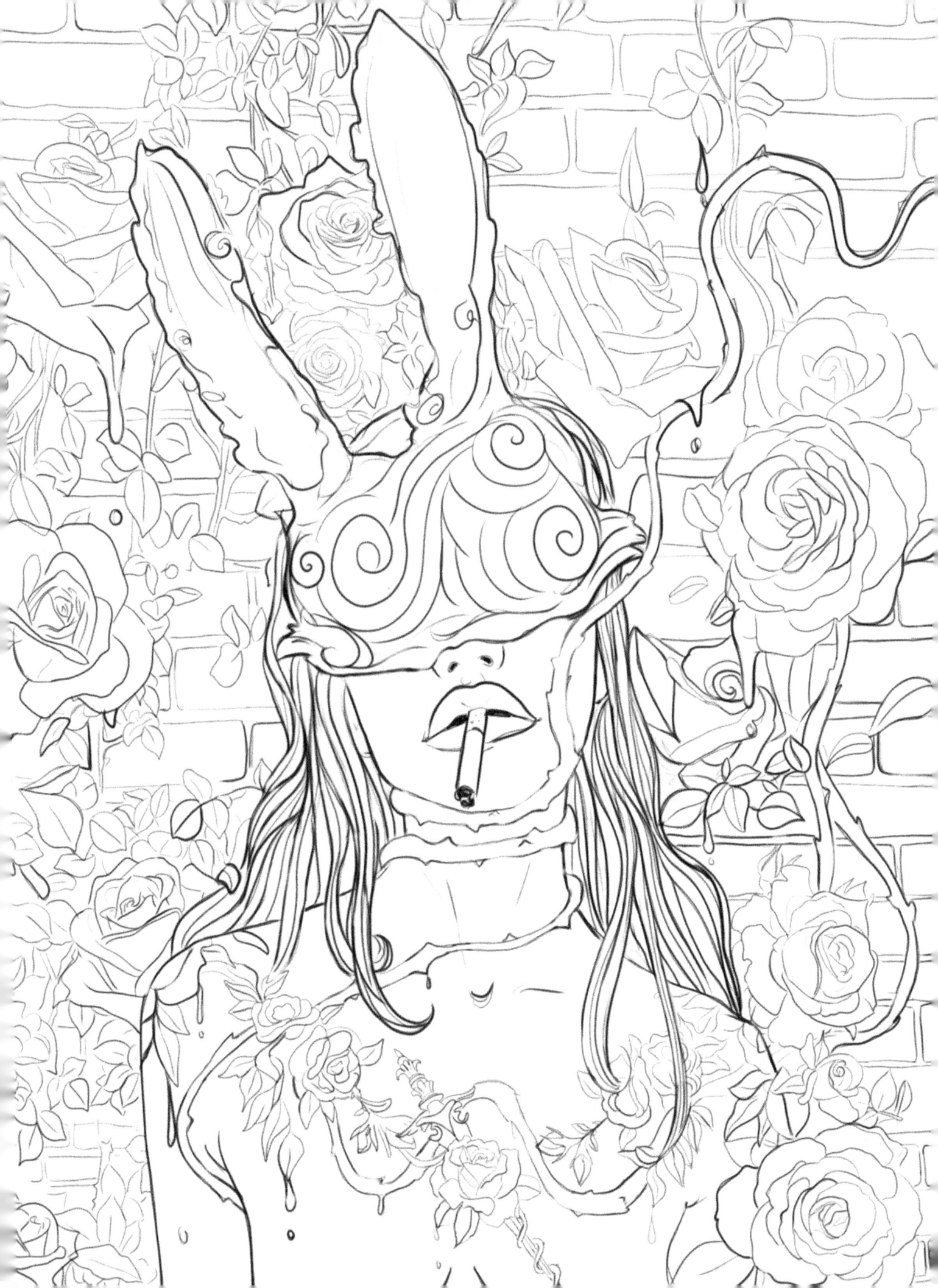

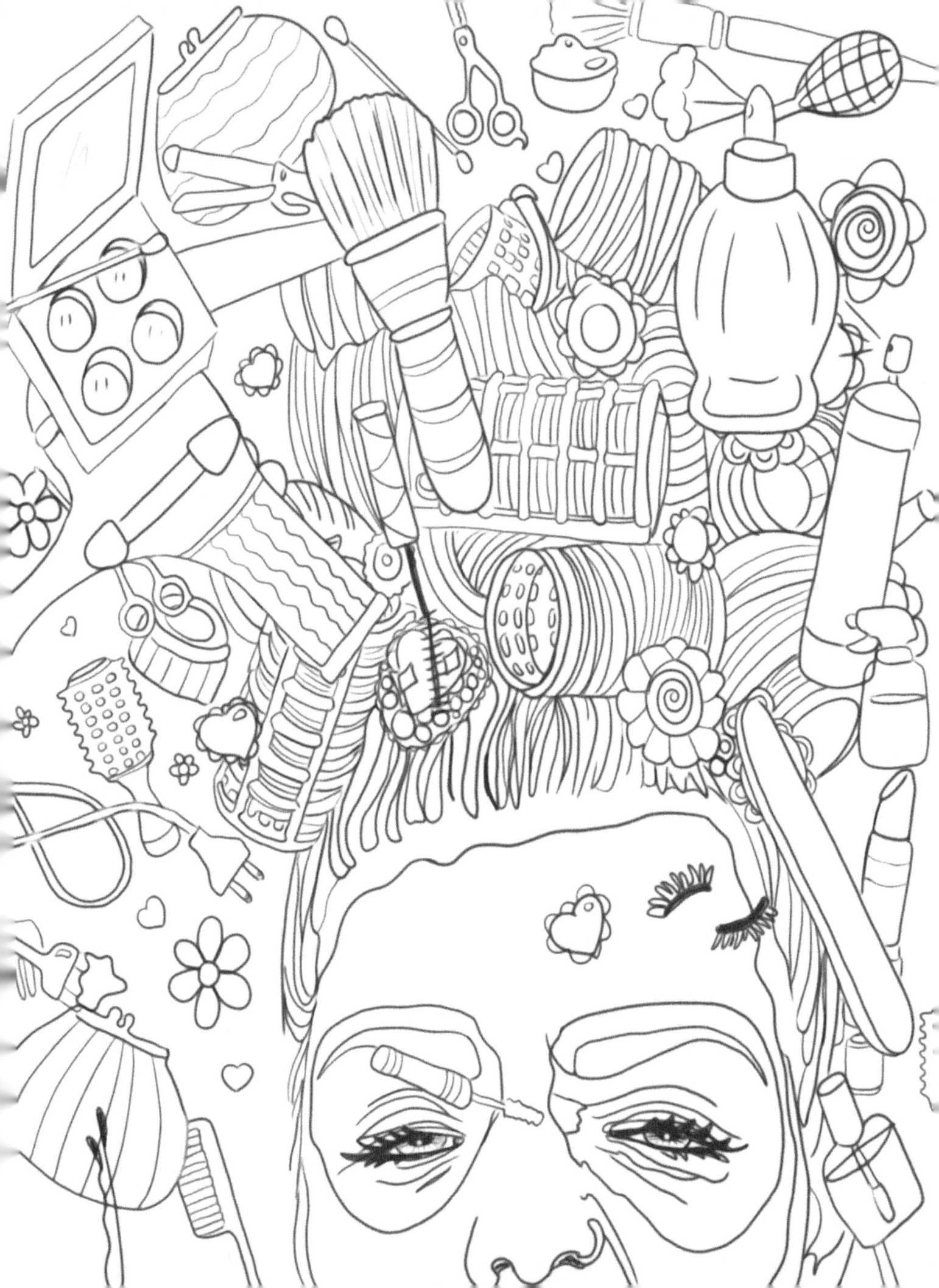

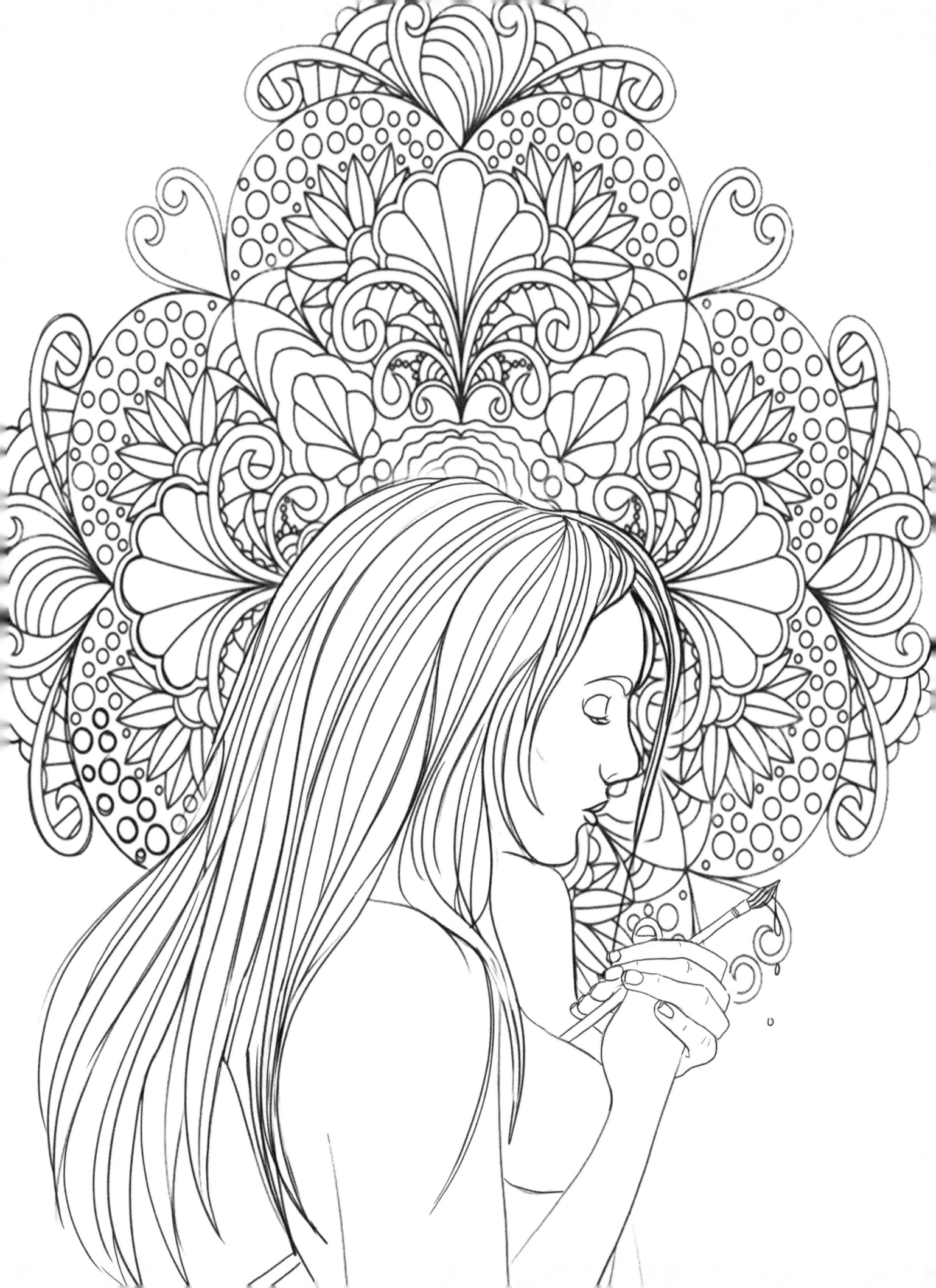

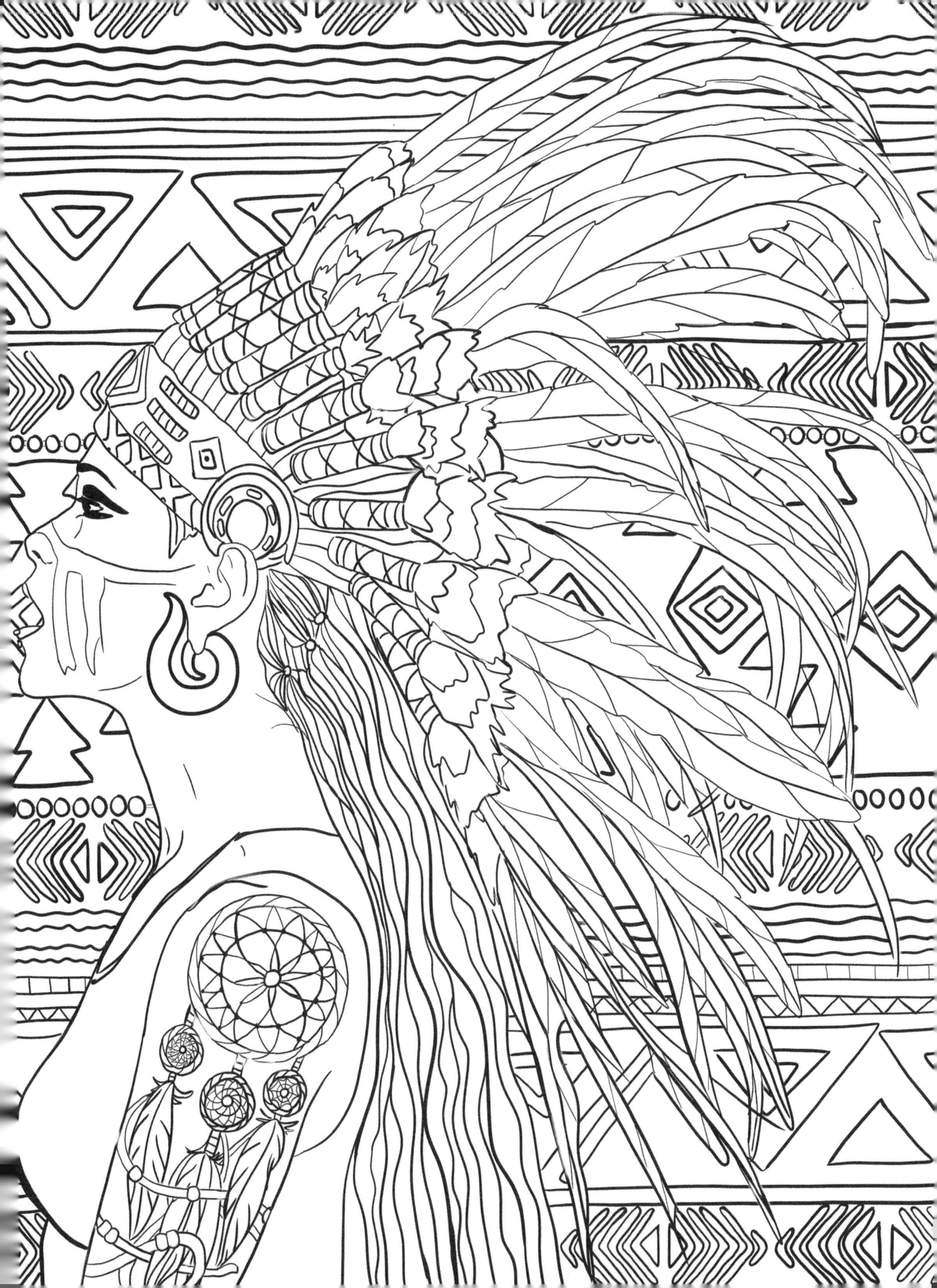

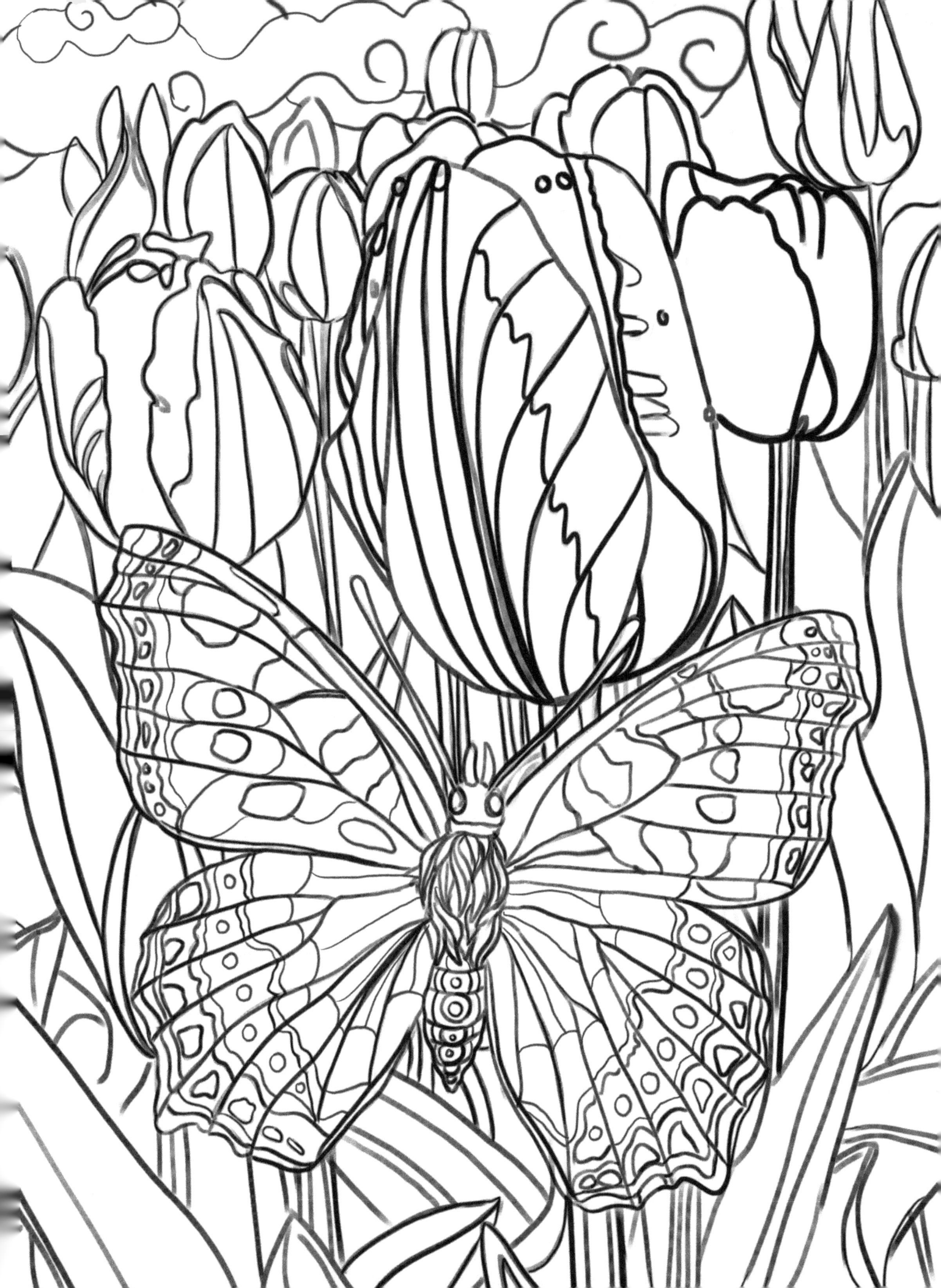

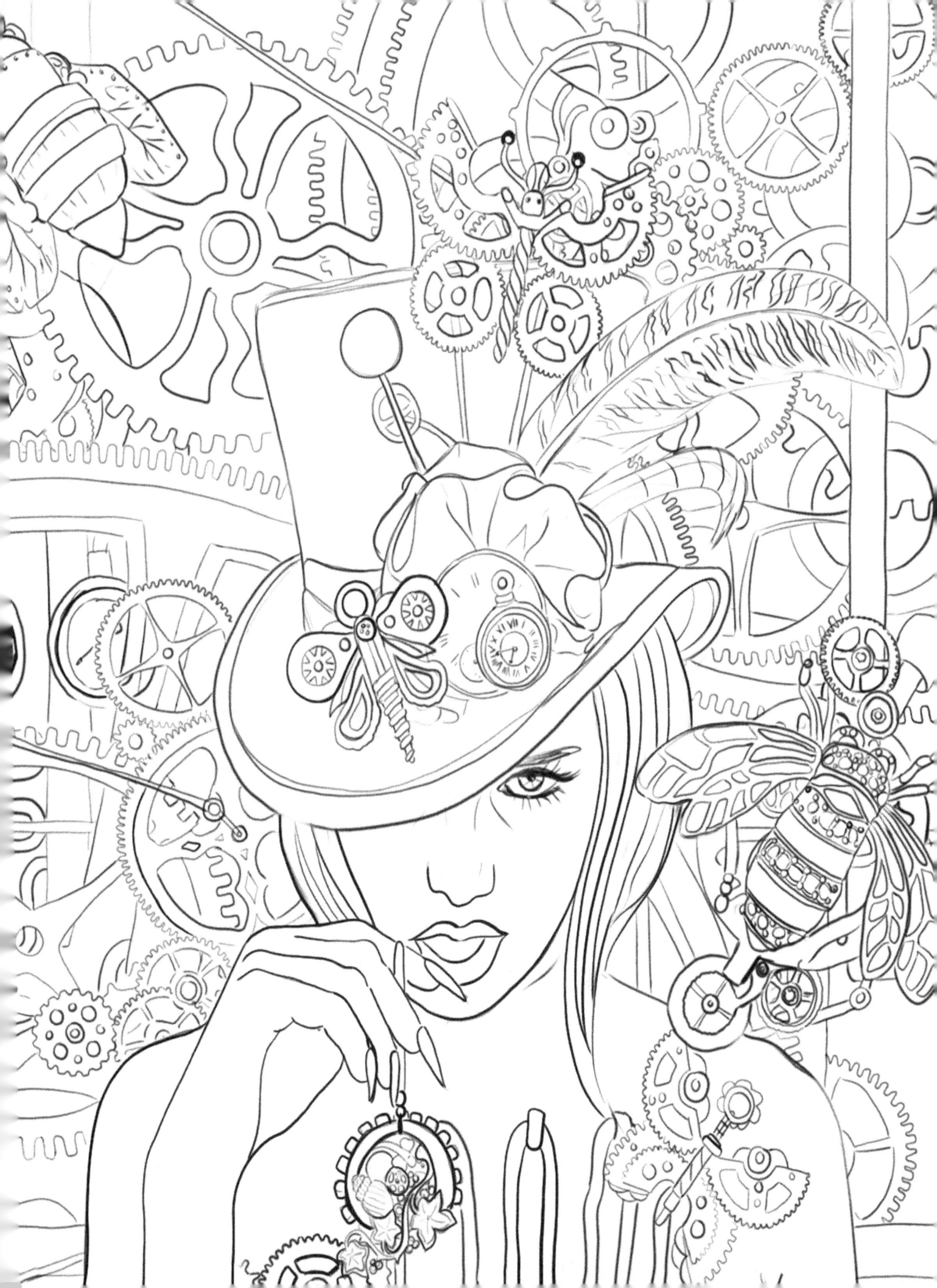

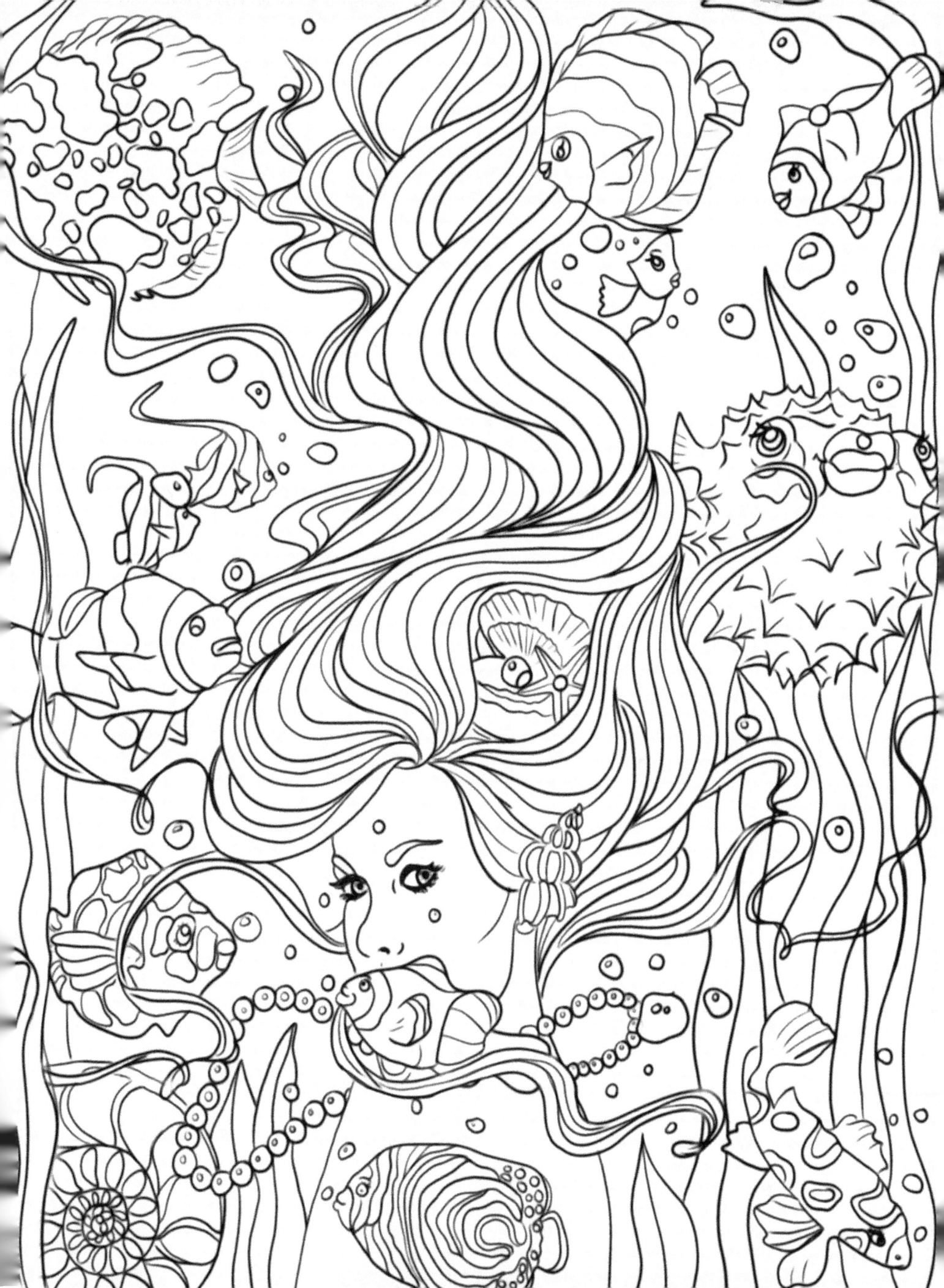

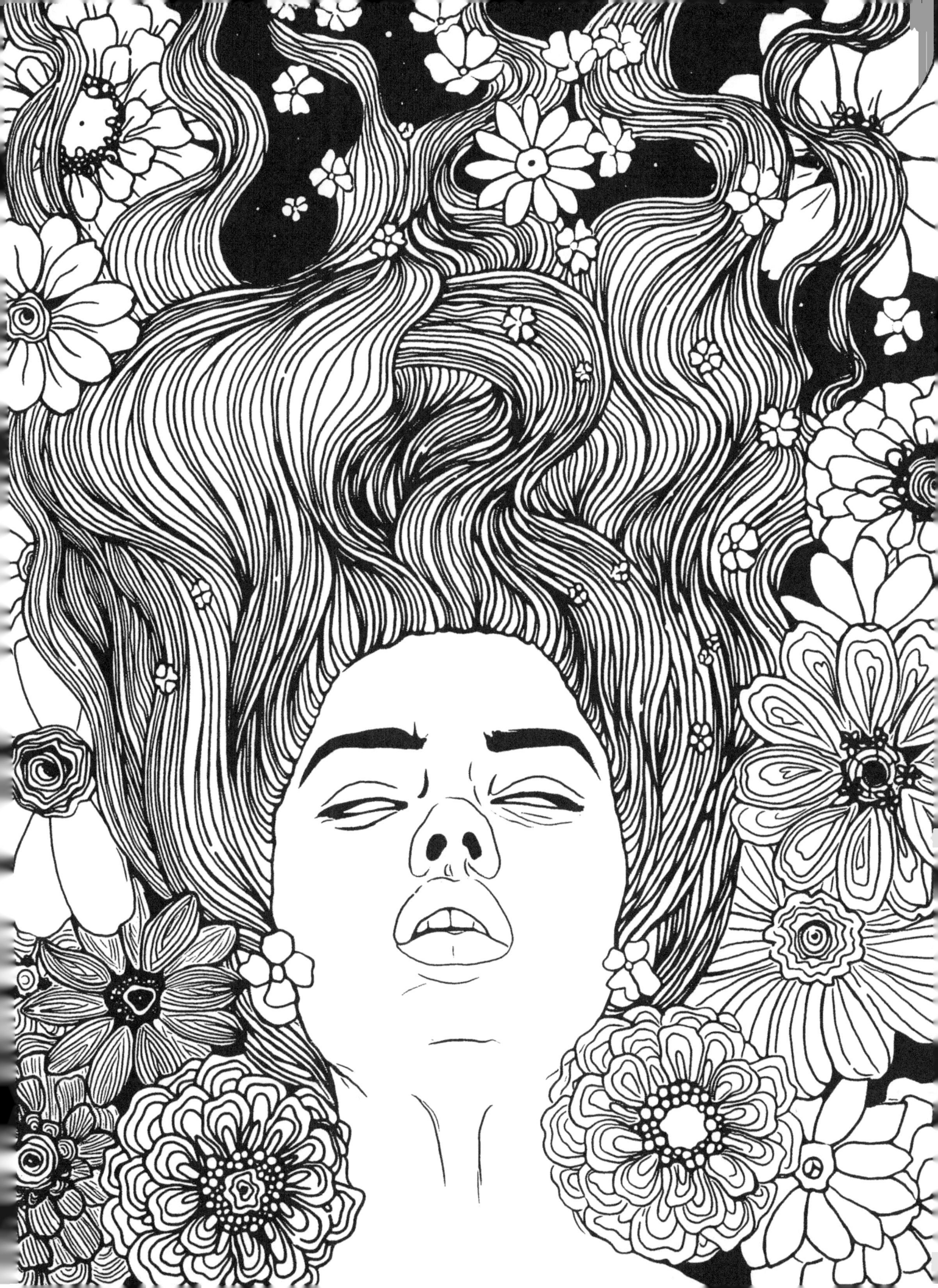

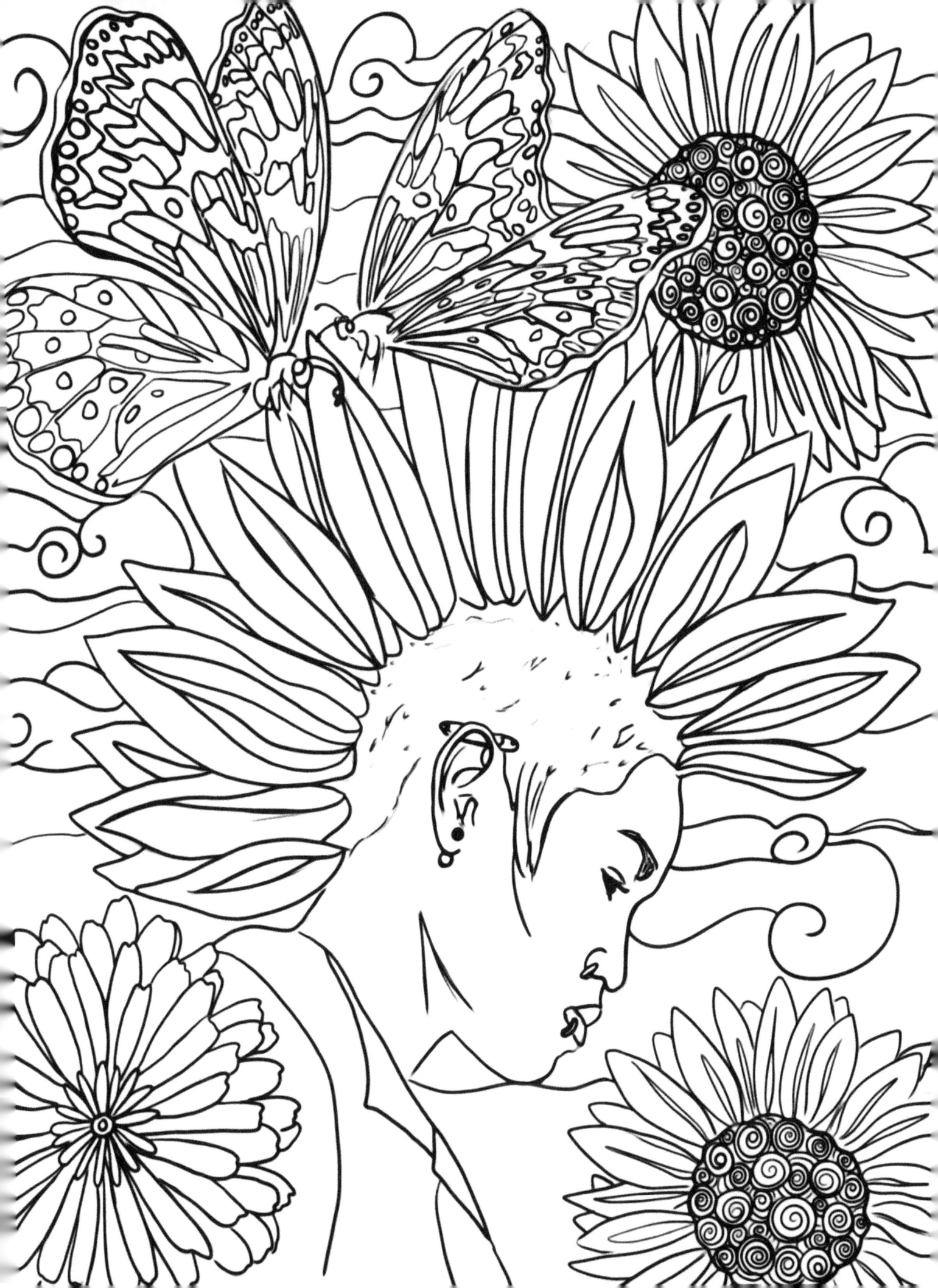

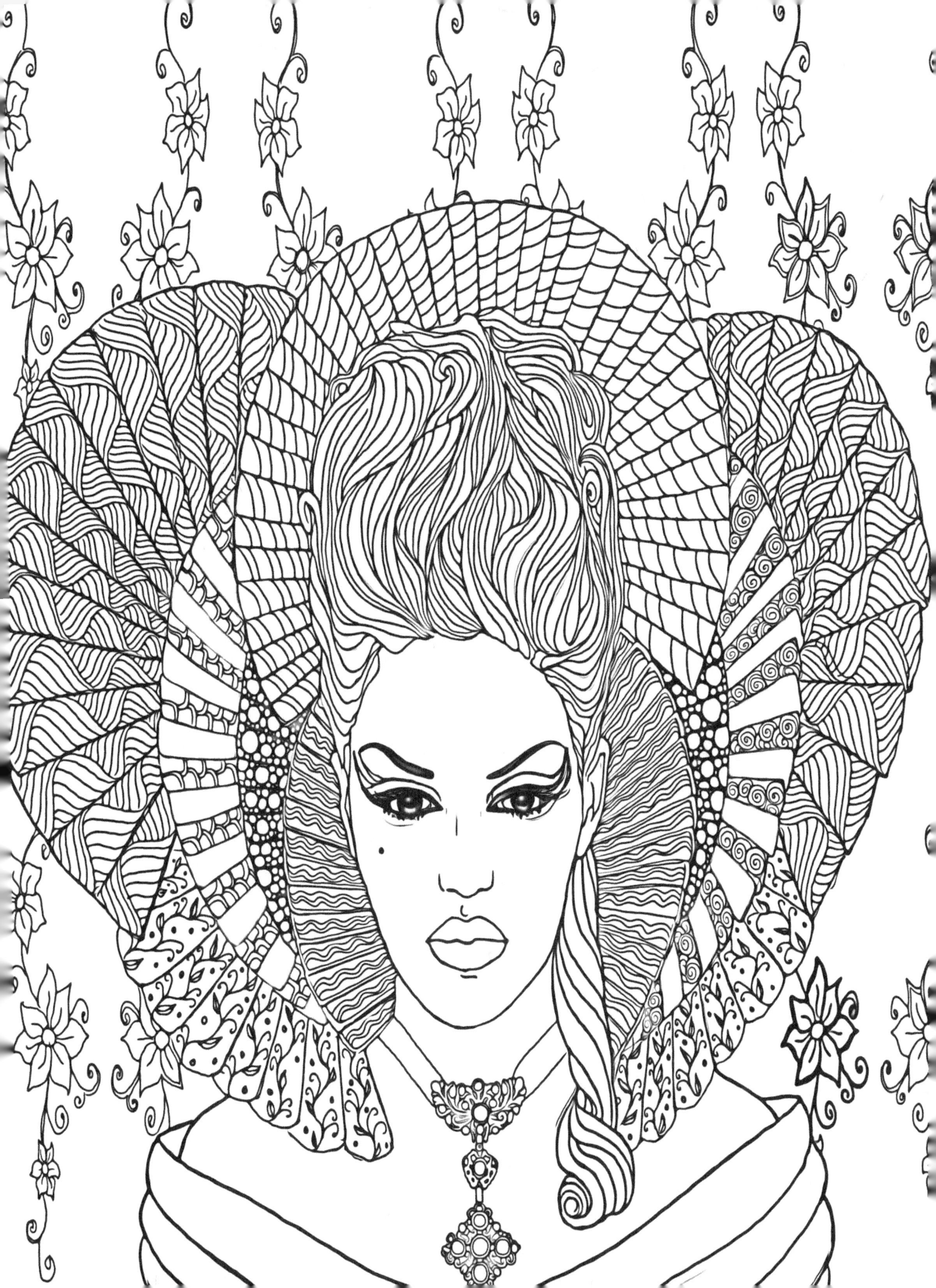

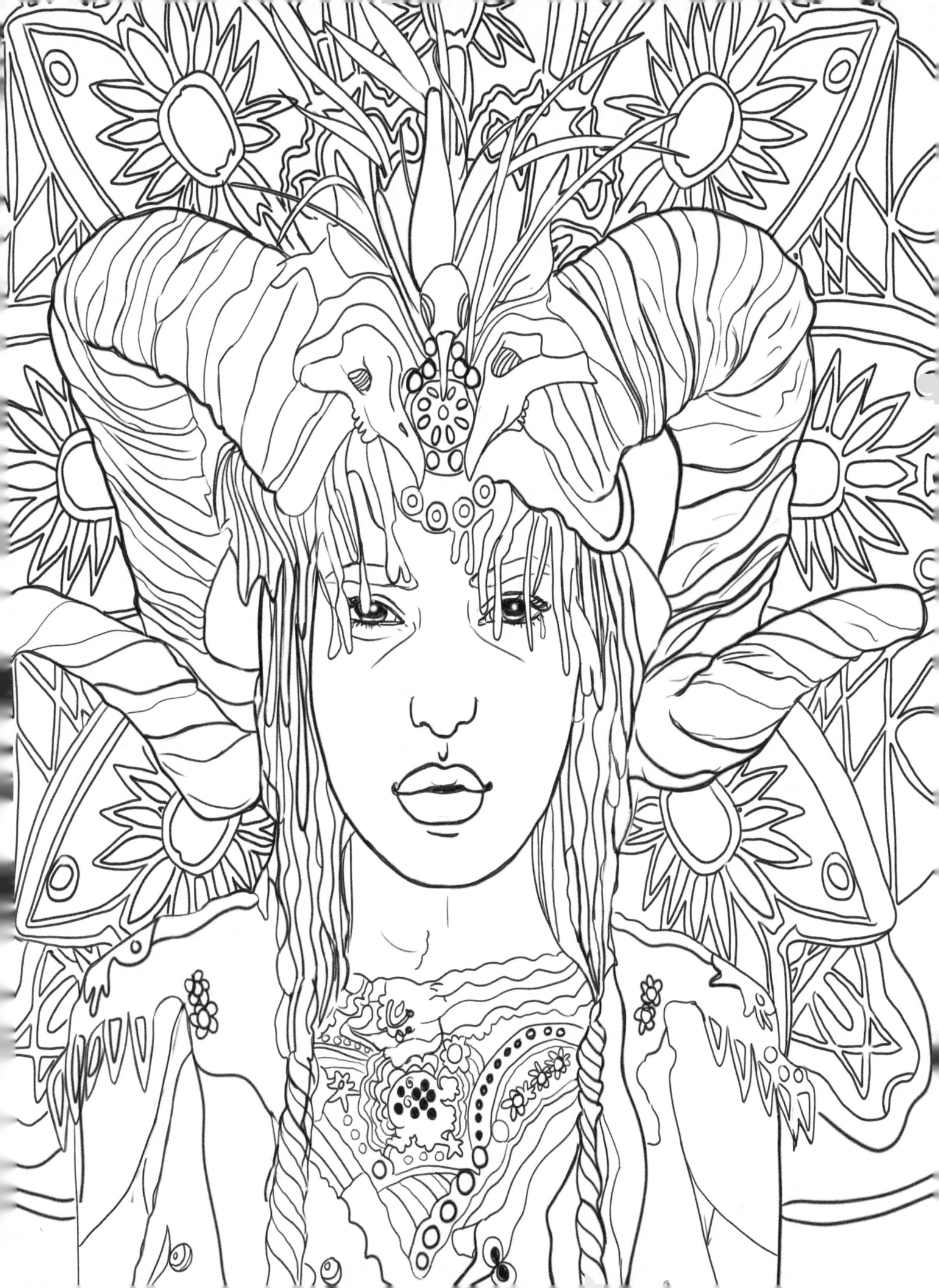

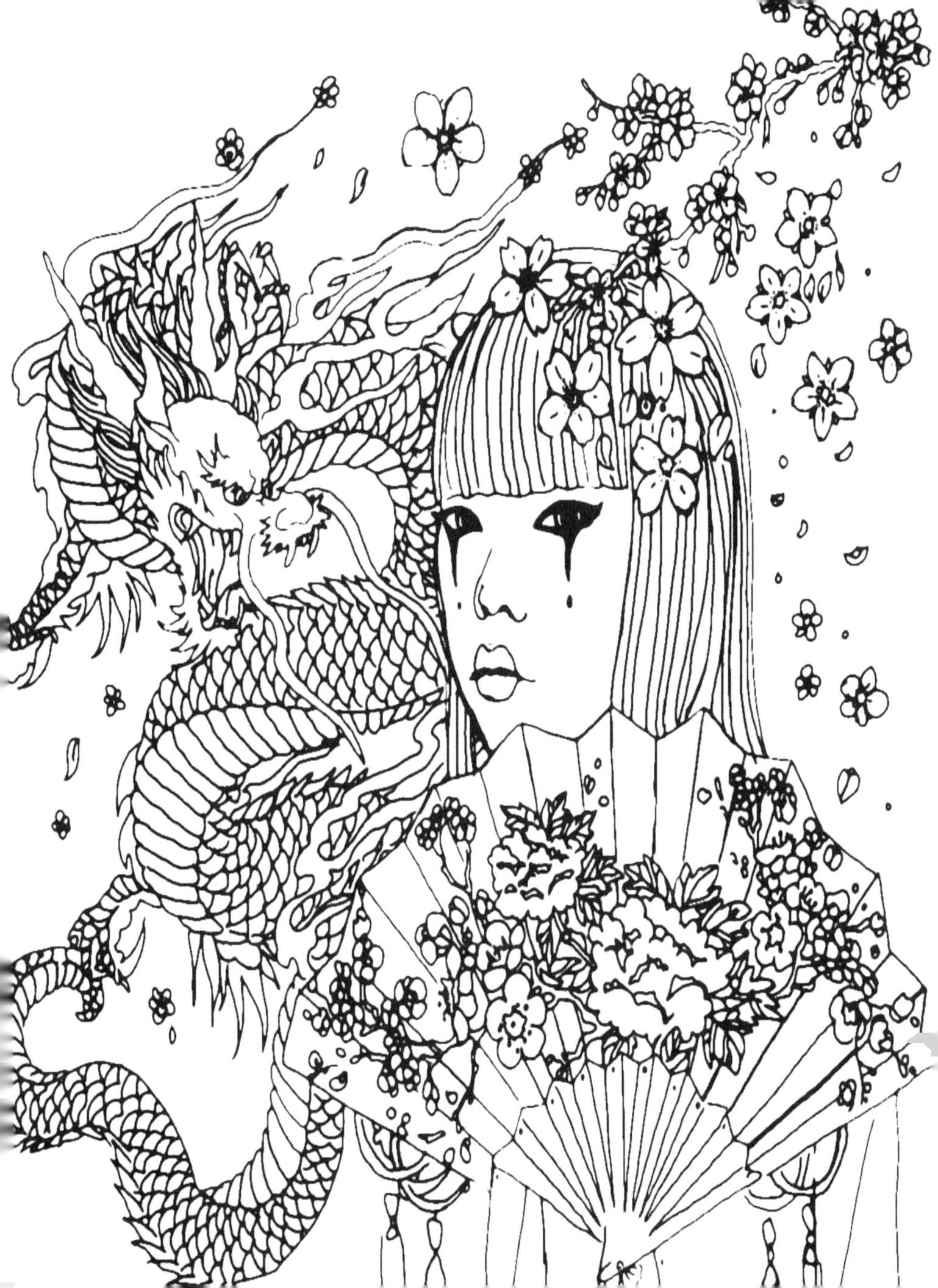

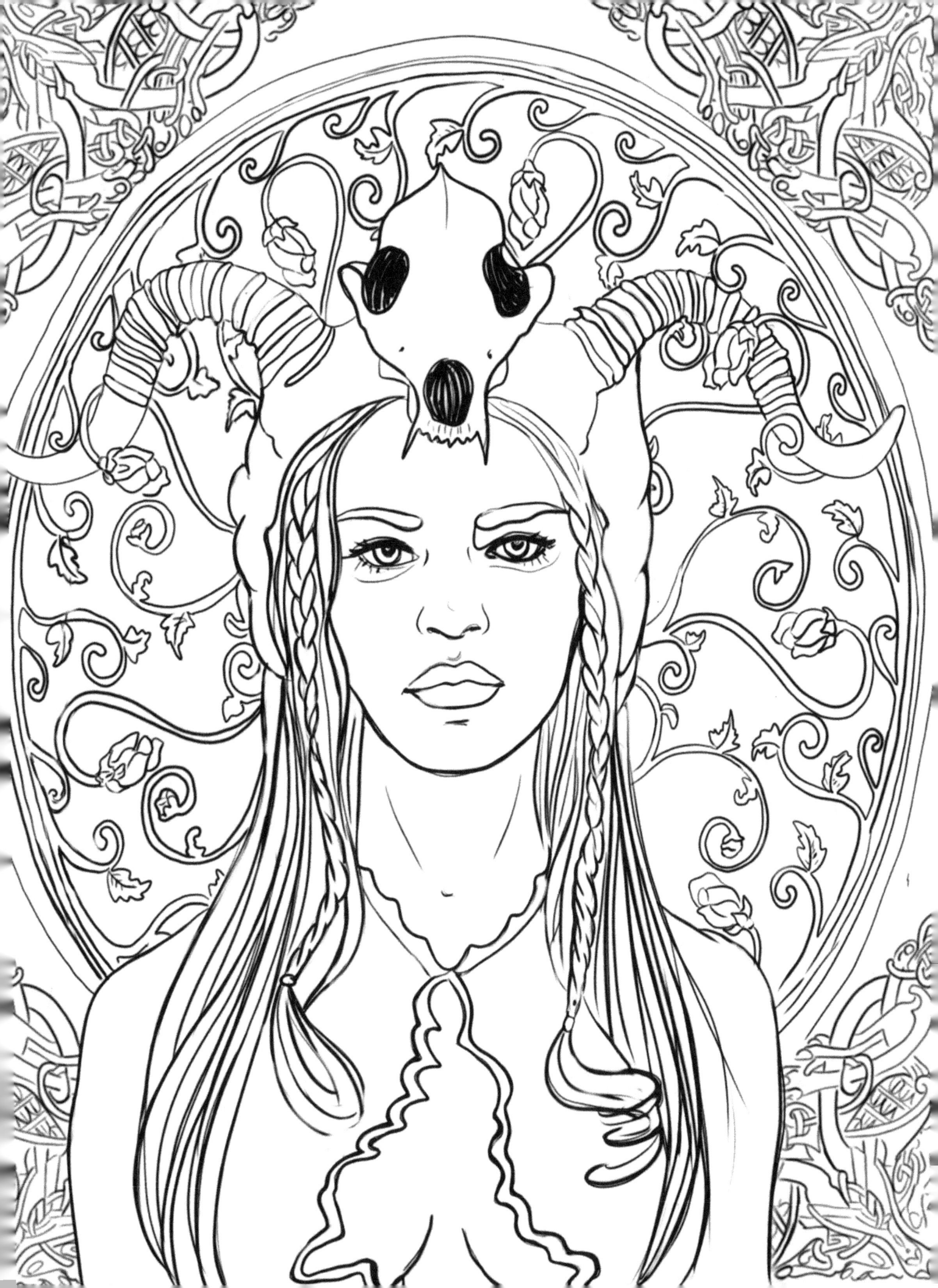

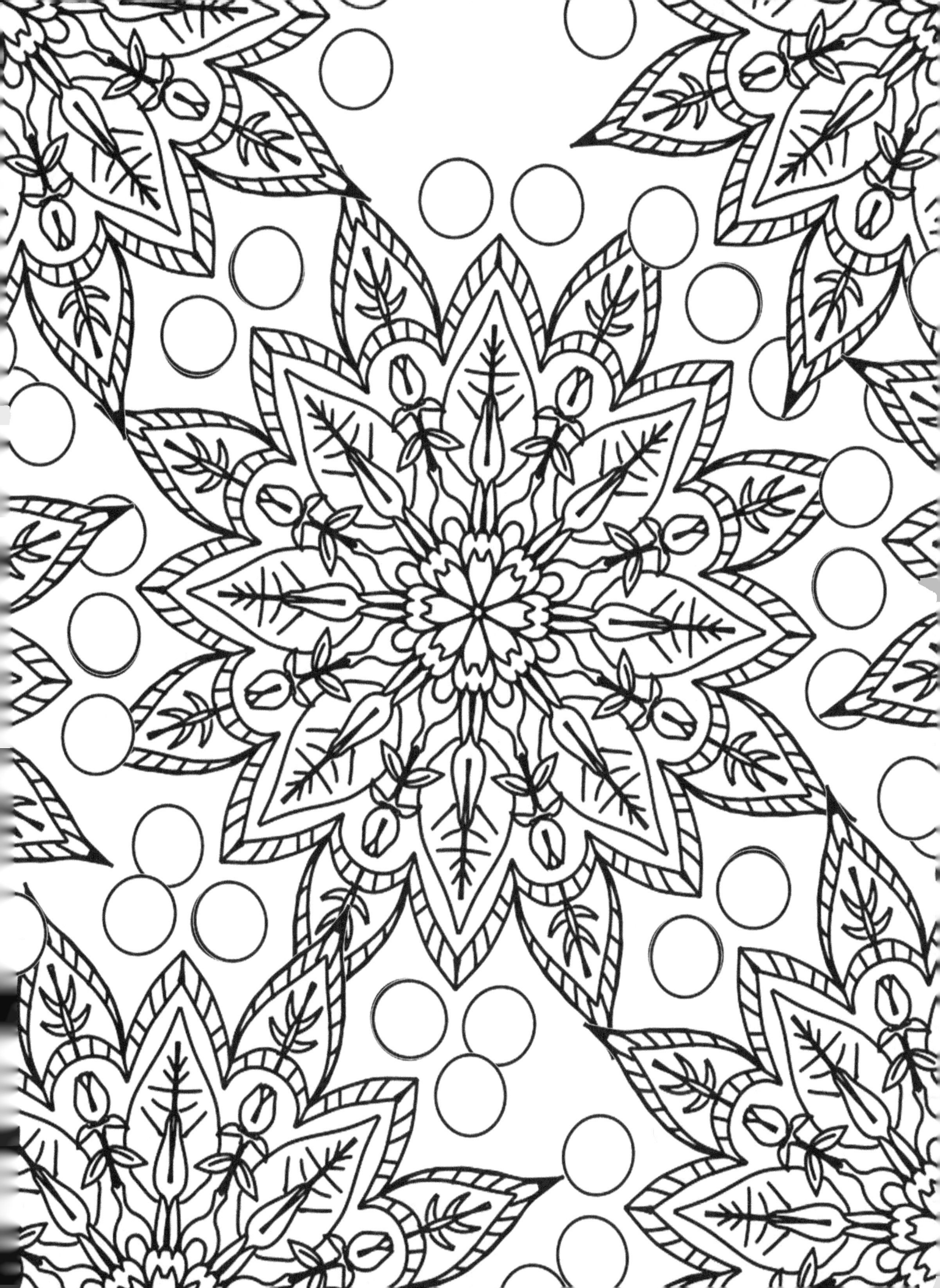

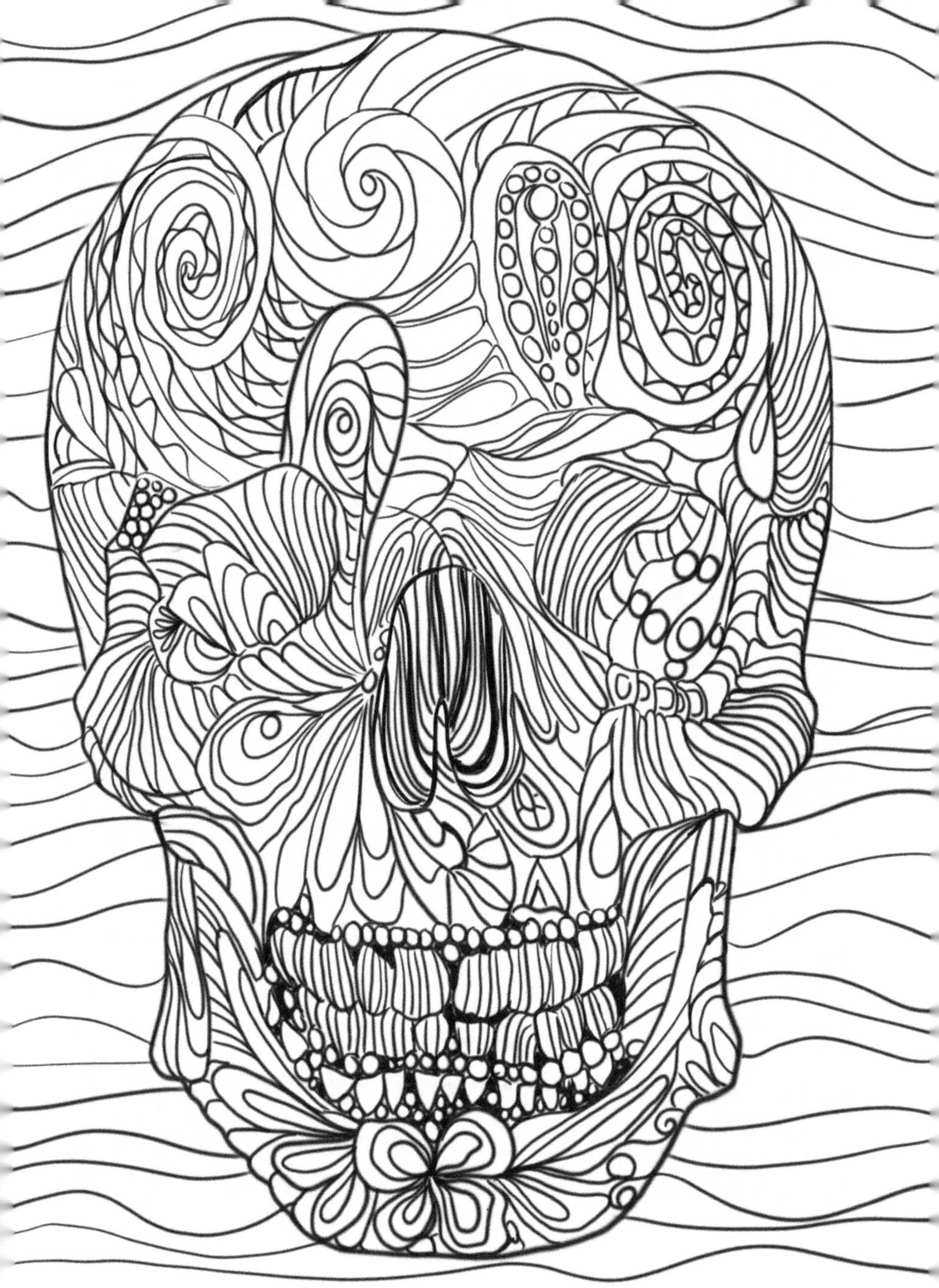

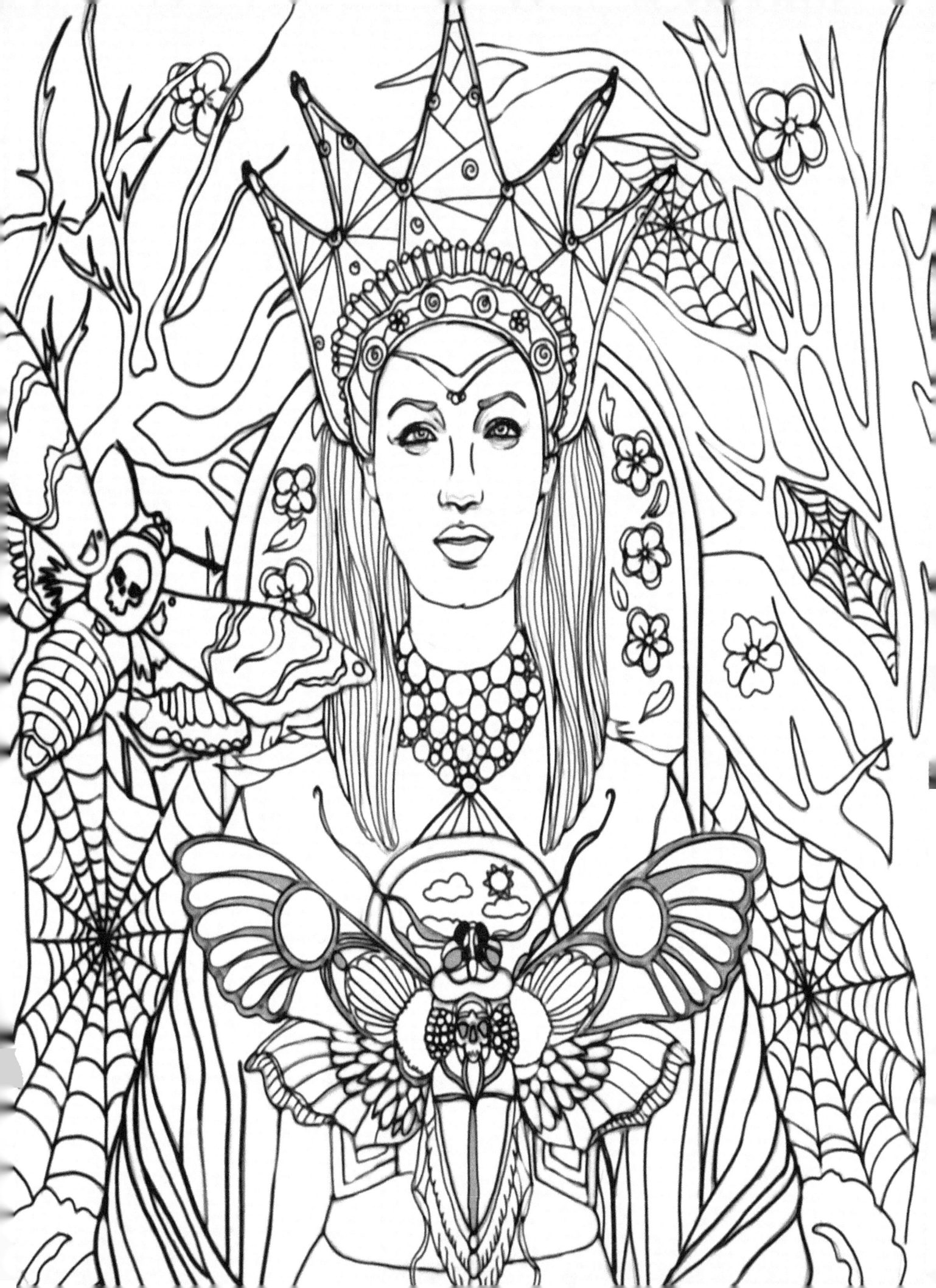

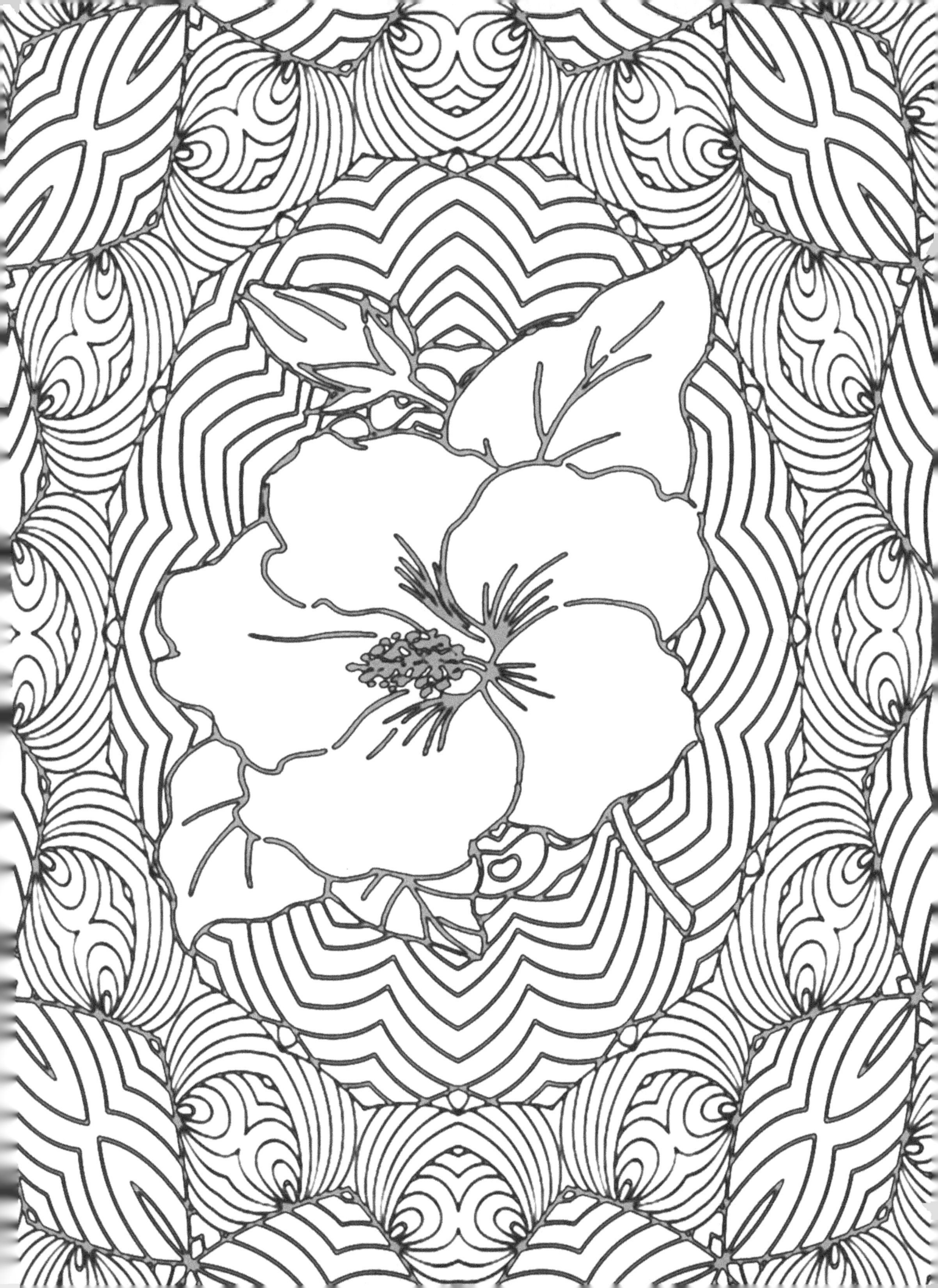

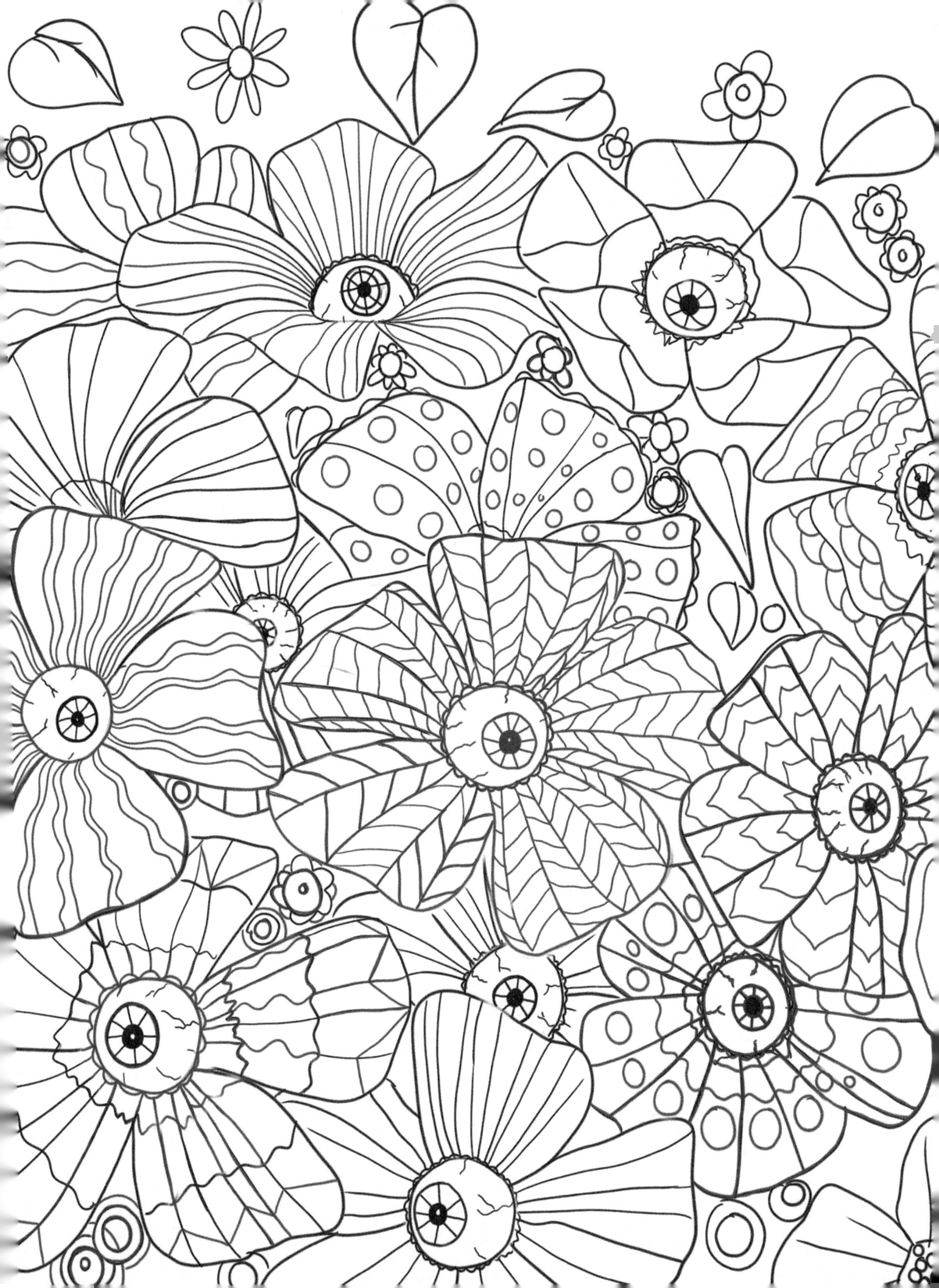

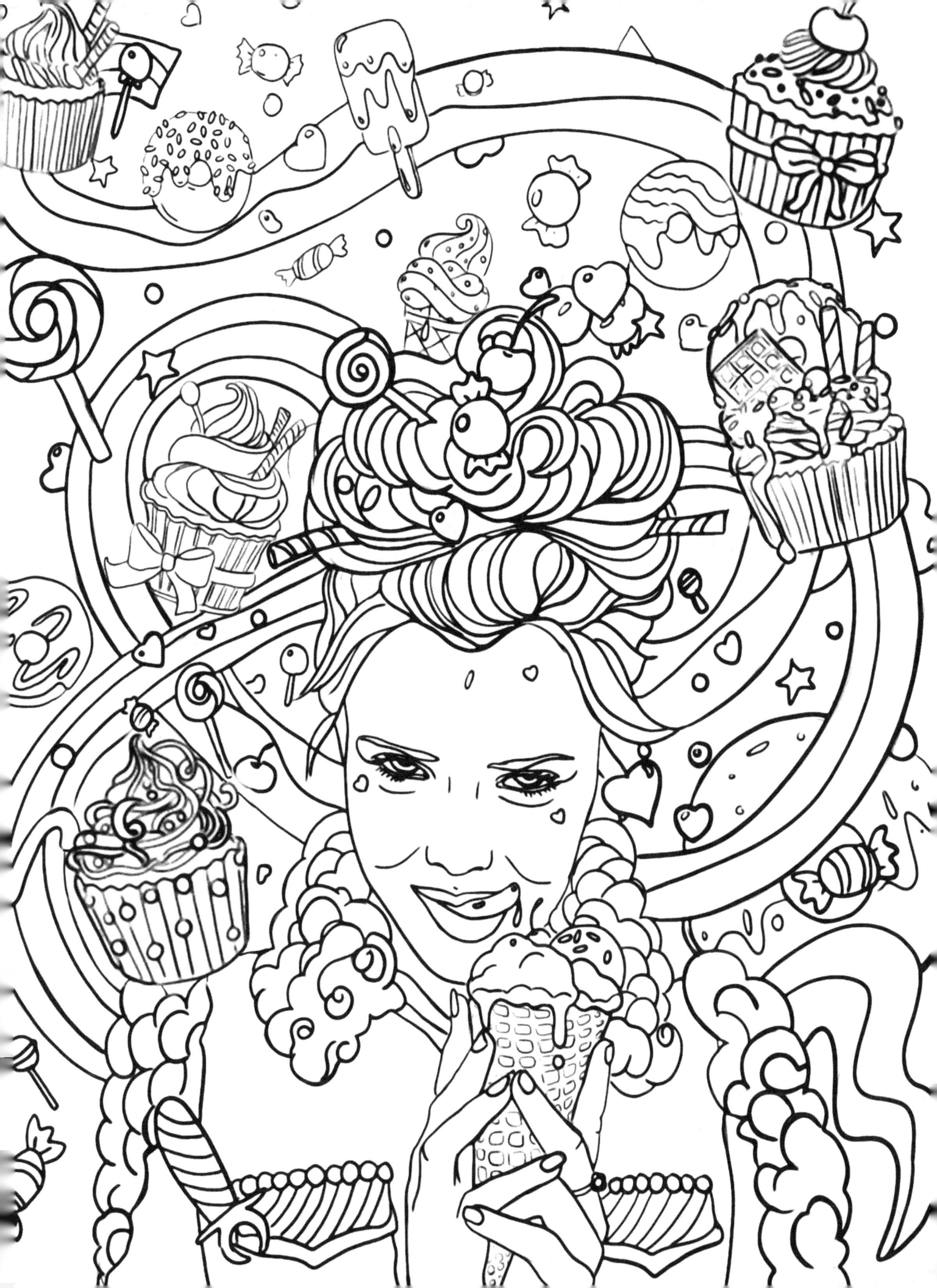

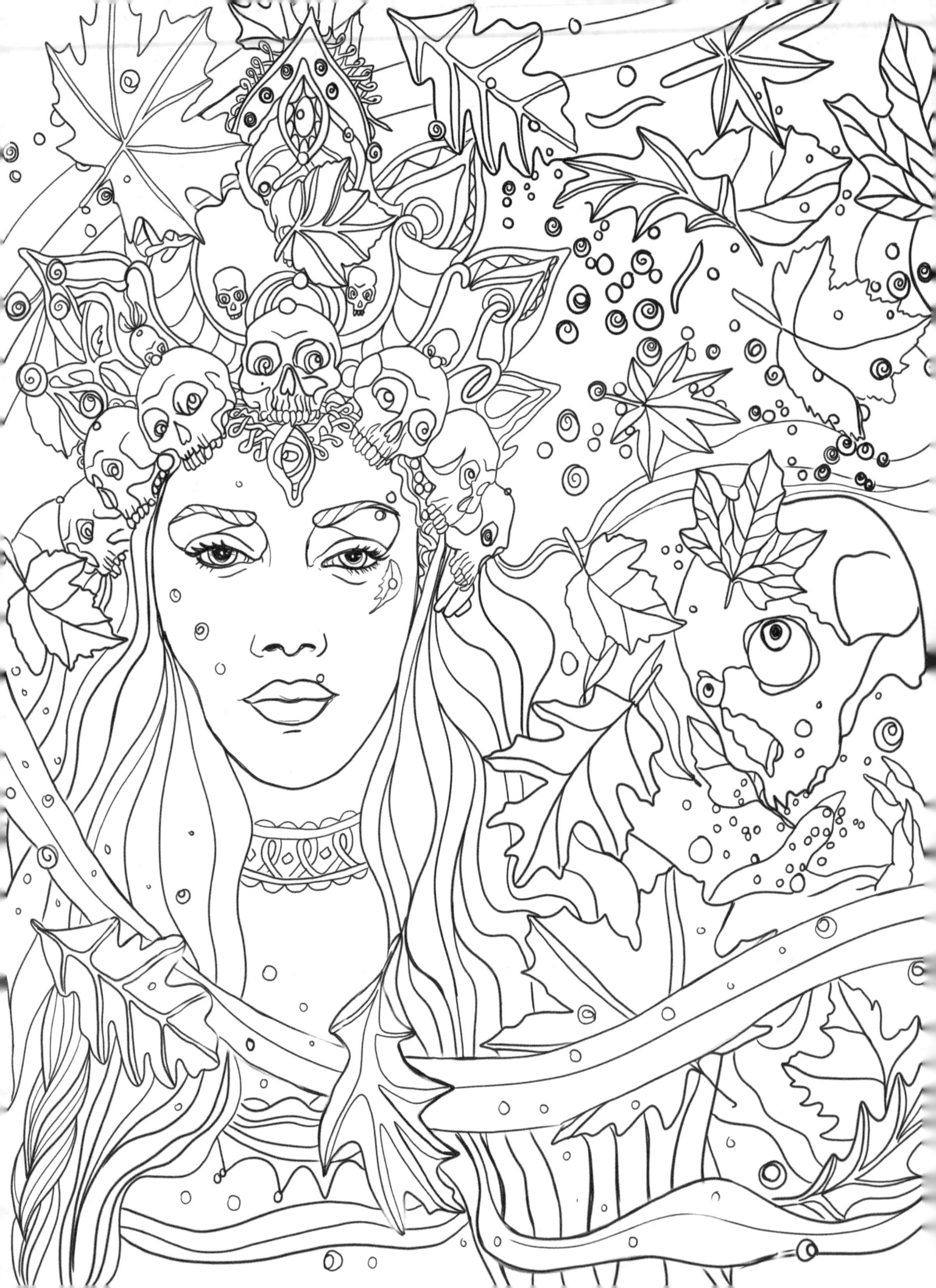

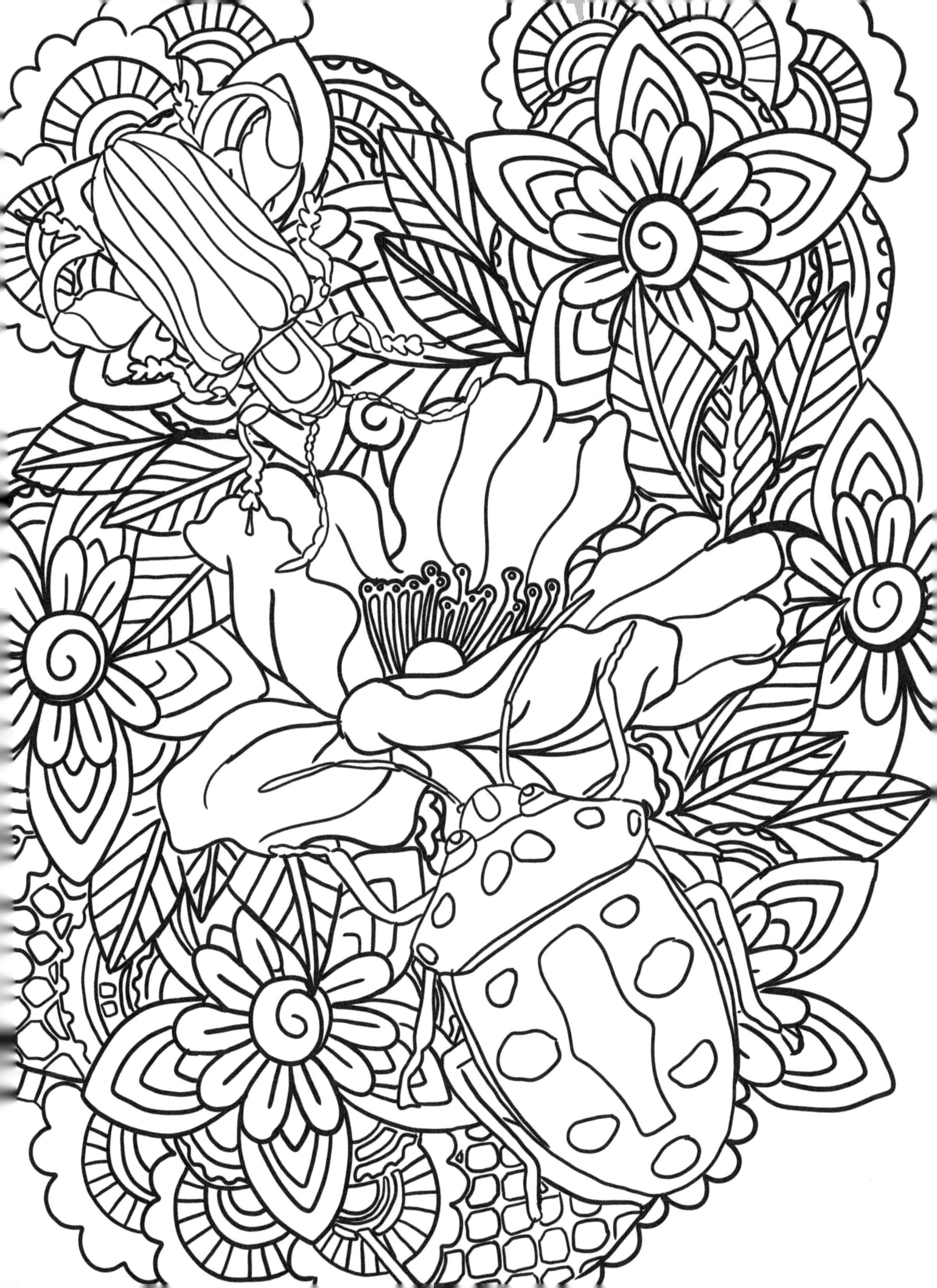

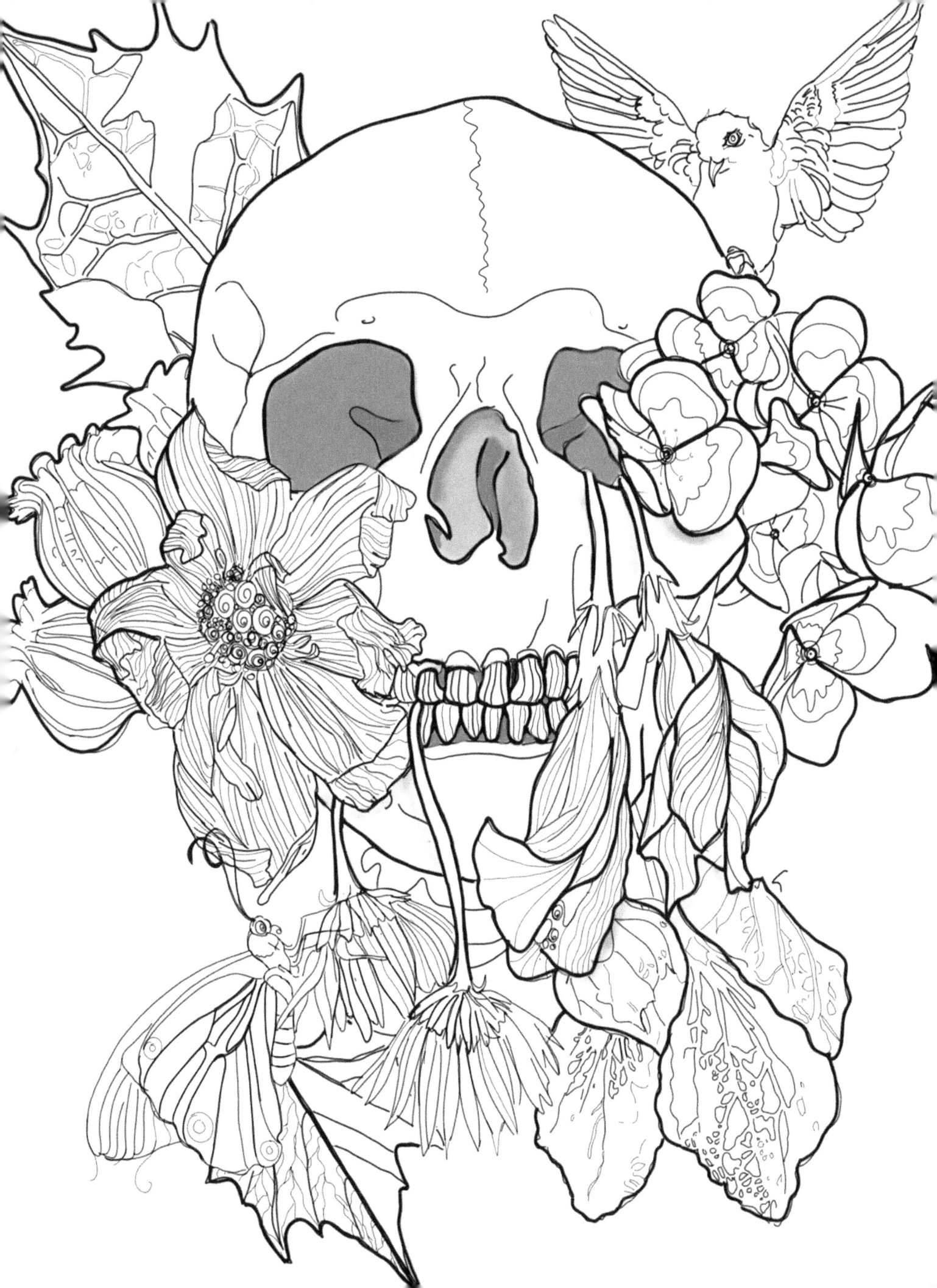

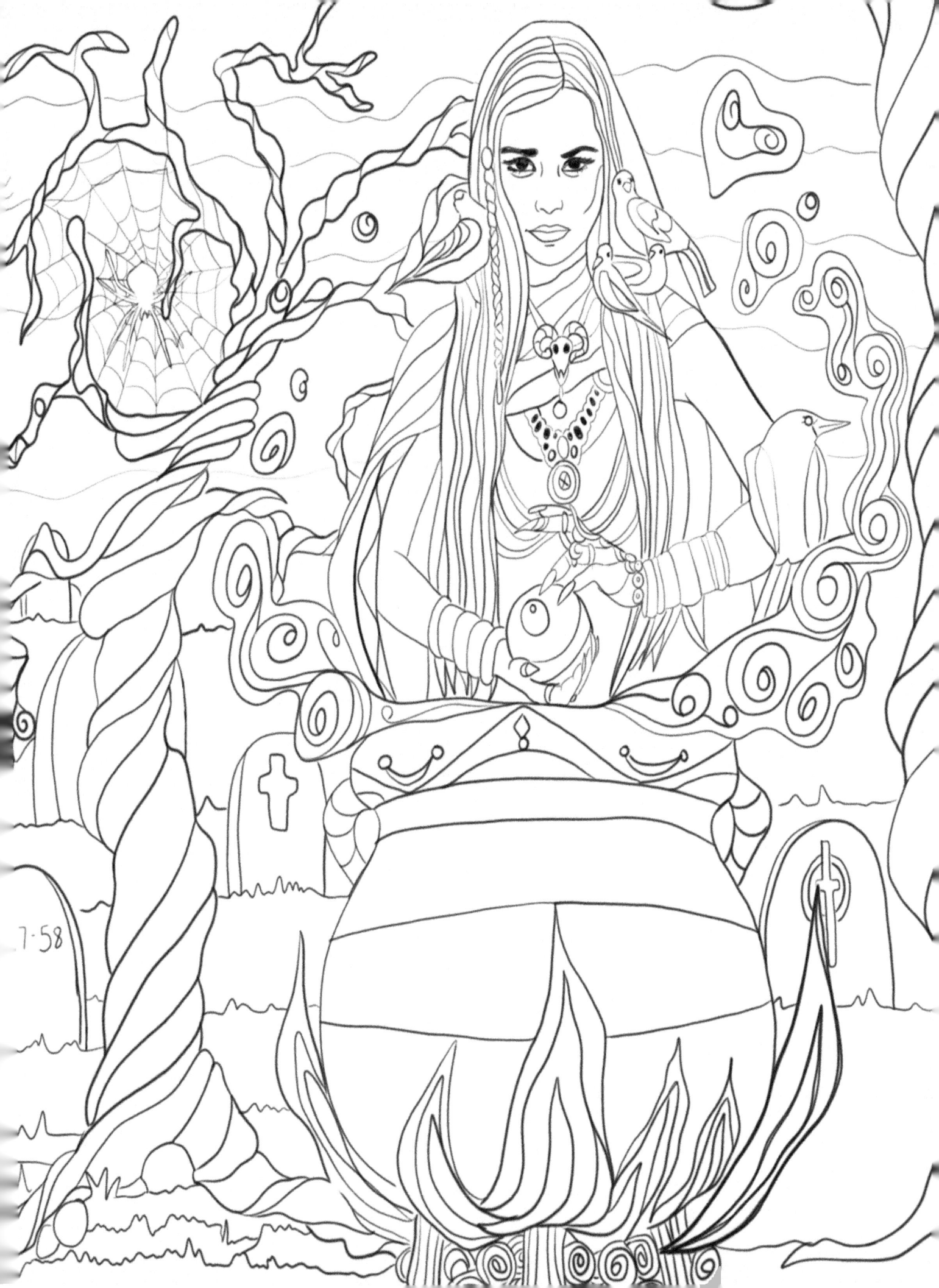

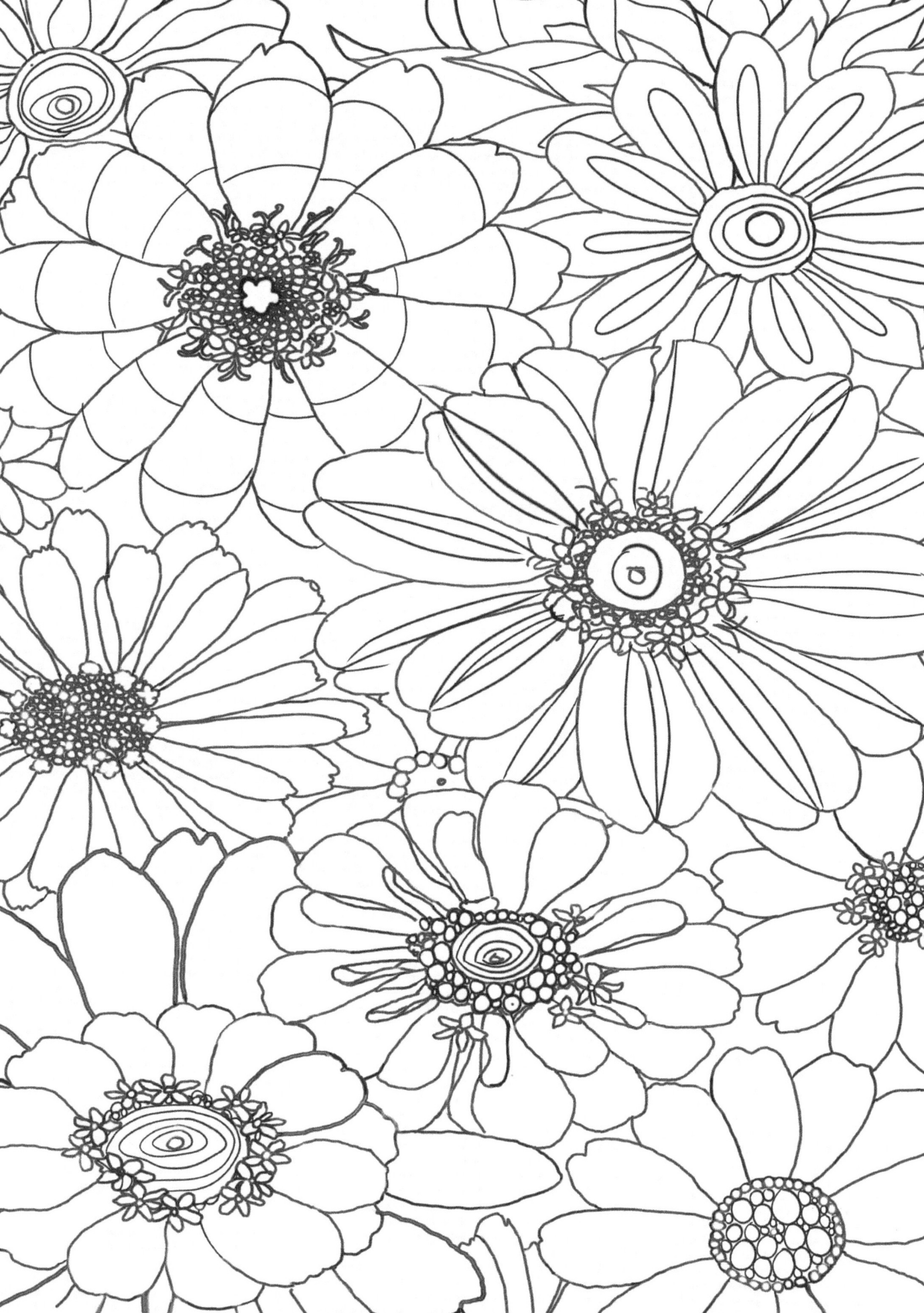

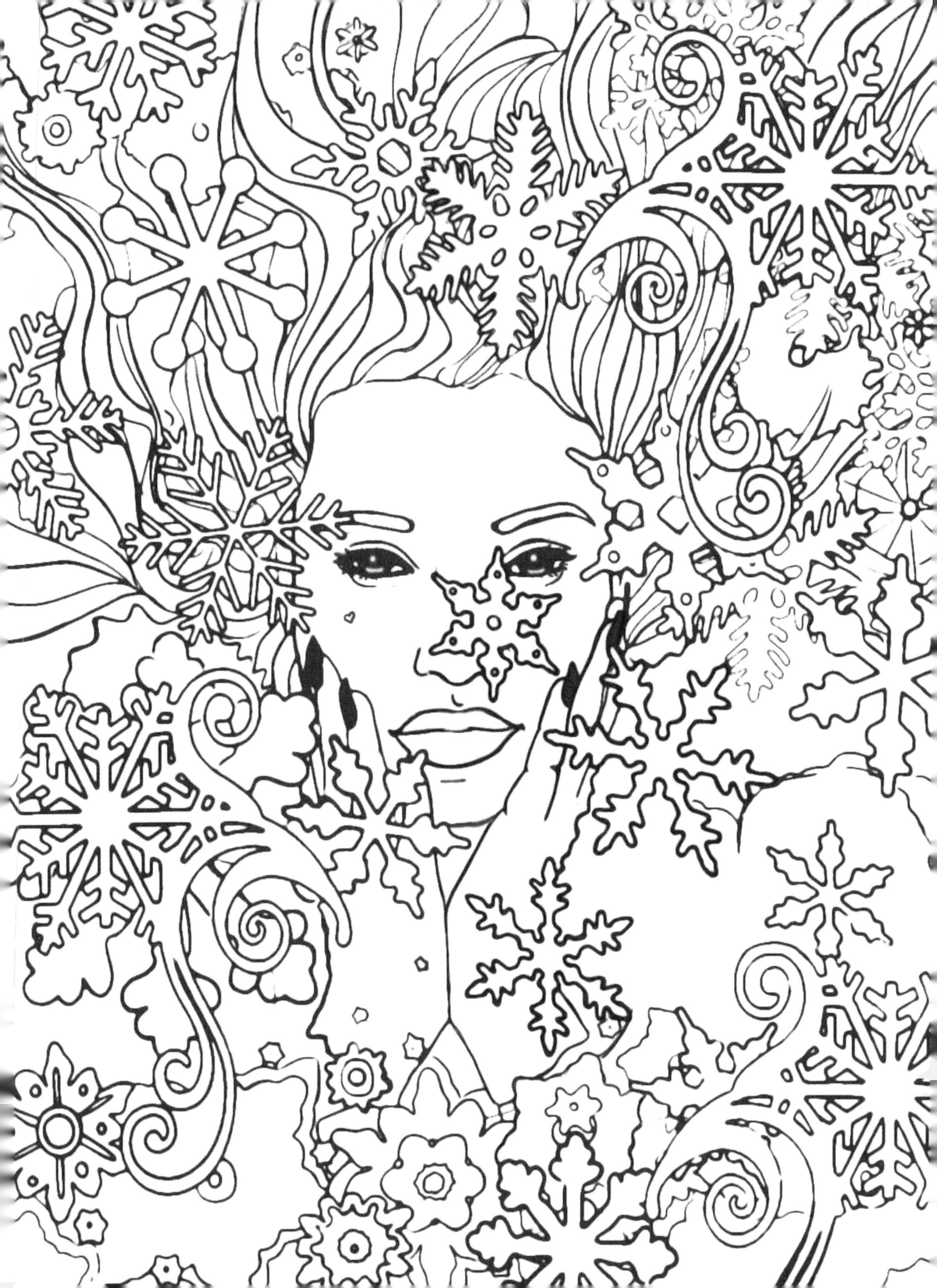

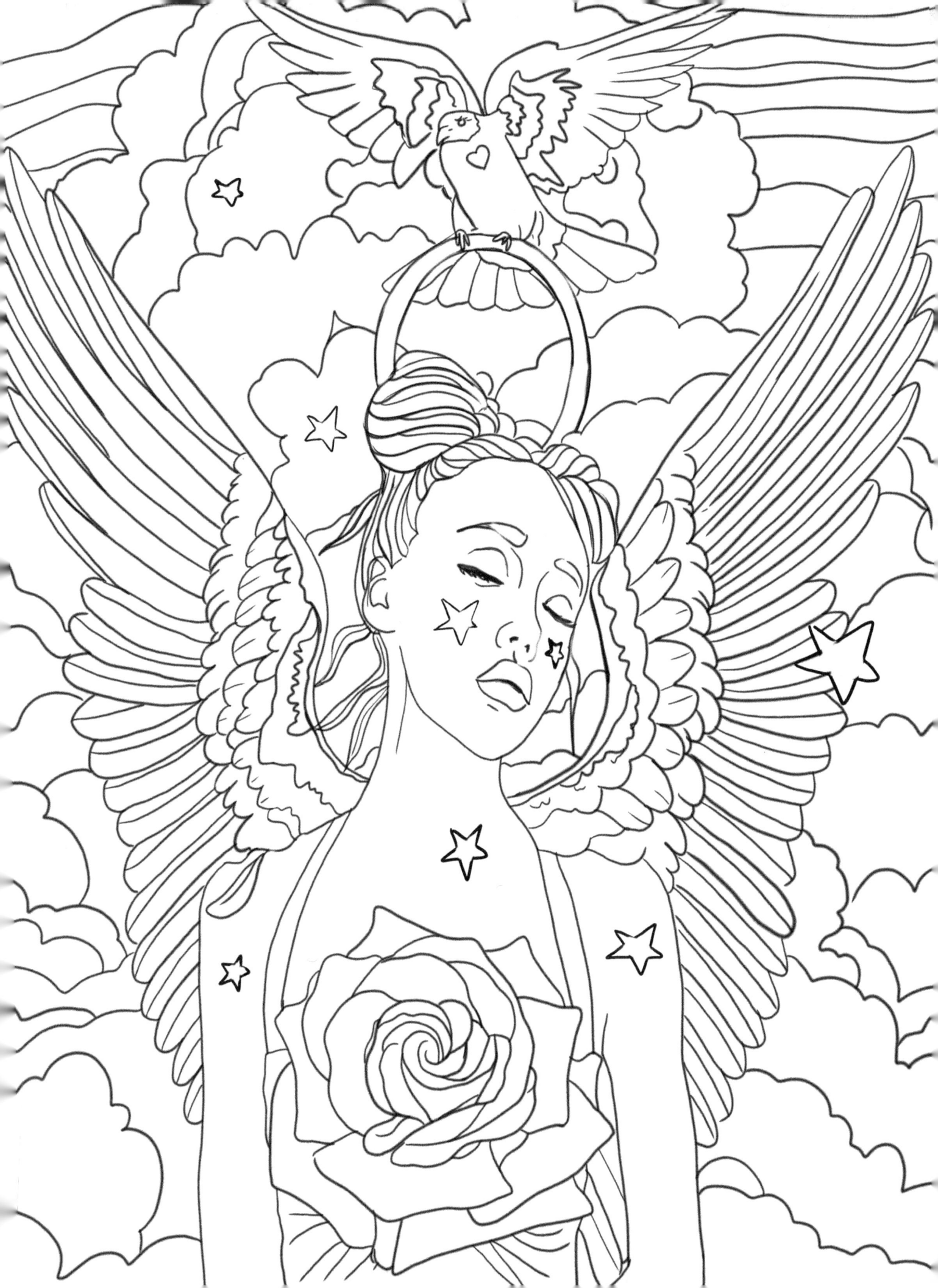

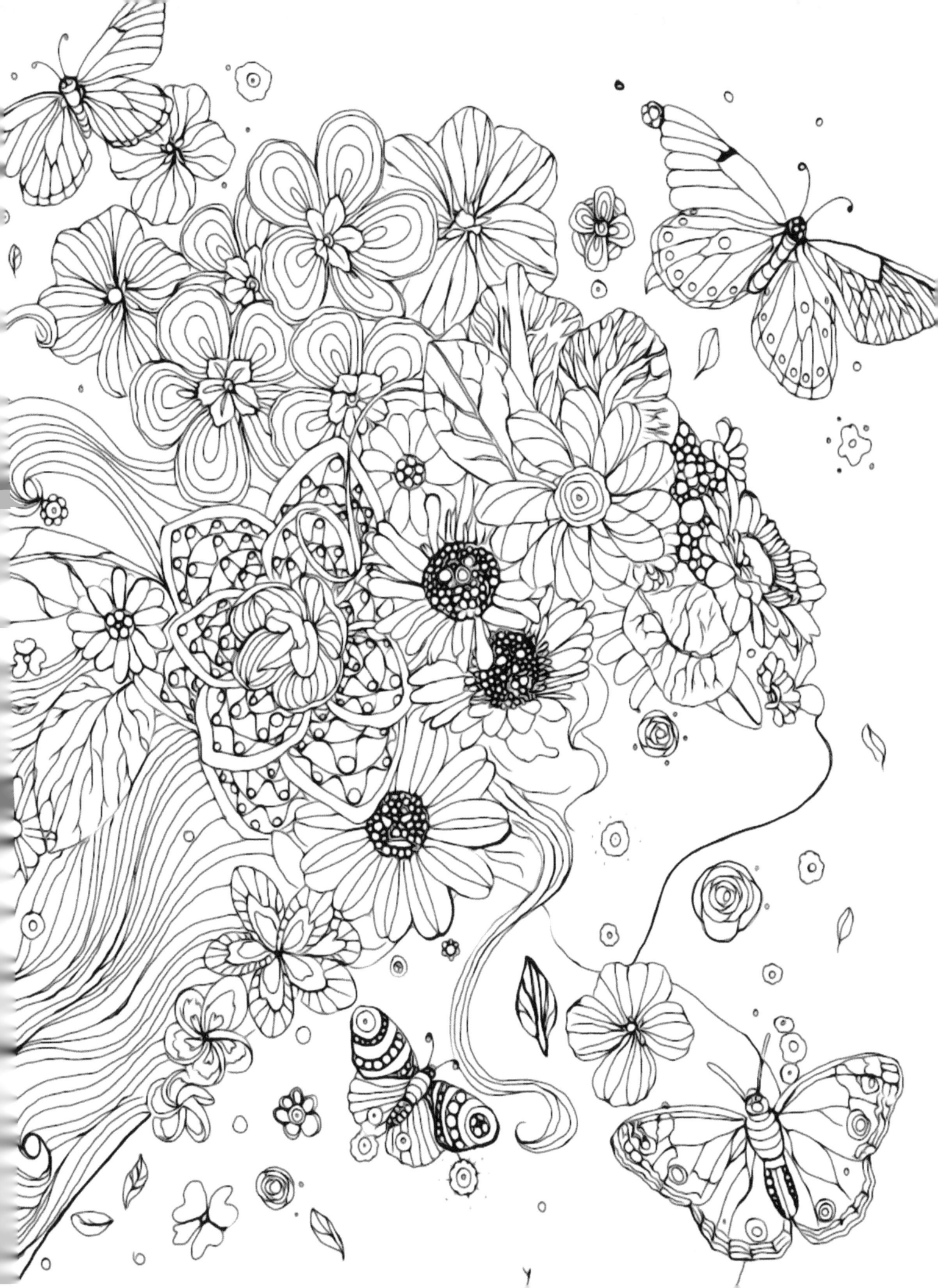

Inspired by my dear friend, Dr. Ali Winters

www.ingramcontent.com/pod-product-compliance
Lightning Source LLC
Chambersburg PA
CBHW062341220526
45469CB00008B/2793